Friends: A Devotional Journal

RUTH HARMS CALKIN

Friends

To Jill —
my daughter —
my friend!
Love —
Mom

Tyndale House Publishers, Inc. Wheaton, Illinois

Visit Tyndale's exciting Web site at www.tyndale.com

Designed by Andrea Gjeldum

Edited by Vinita Wright

Scripture quotations are taken from the *Holy Bible,* New Living Translation, copyright © 1996. Used by permission of Tyndale House Publishers, Inc., Wheaton, Illinois 60189. All rights reserved.

ISBN 0-8423-1094-0

Printed in the United States of America

03 02 01 00 99 98 97
7 6 5 4 3 2 1

To my cherished friends:

Through the tested years our friendship proves

to be another joyful way of knowing God.

I love being friends with you!

CONTENTS

PART FIVE: Our Greatest Friend

IN HIS GREAT WISDOM, GOD

FORESAW THE NEEDS OF OUR HEARTS. HE SAW HOW OFTEN WE WOULD NEED SOMEONE WITH WHOM WE COULD SHARE OUR THOUGHTS, OUR SECRET DREAMS, OUR LAUGHTER, AND OUR TEARS. WE WOULD NEED SOMEONE WHO WOULD ACCEPT US FOR WHO WE ARE, NOT FOR WHAT WE DO. SOMEONE WHO WOULD UNDERSTAND US BETTER THAN ANYONE ELSE.

GOD KNEW THERE WOULD BE TIMES WHEN WE WOULD BECOME WEARY AND DISCOURAGED, WHEN WE WOULD NEED SOMEONE TO HELP KEEP OUR HOPE ALIVE. WE WOULD NEED PEOPLE WHO WOULD ENCOURAGE US TO MAKE CORRECTIONS AND PRAISE US FOR OUR ACCOMPLISHMENTS.

FOR ALL THESE REASONS, GOD GAVE US FRIENDS.

SO OFTEN THROUGH THE YEARS GOD HAS SMILED AT ME, DELIGHTED ME, AND LOVED ME THROUGH MY TREASURED FRIENDS—PEOPLE WHO HAVE LEFT AN ETERNAL IMPRINT ON MY LIFE.

IN WAYS BIG AND SMALL I AM CONSTANTLY REMINDED OF HOW VALUABLE MY FRIENDS ARE TO ME. FRIENDS WHO NEVER BETRAY A TRUST. FRIENDS WHO WARM MY WORLD WITH THOUGHTFULNESS AND UNDERSTANDING.

FRIENDS WHO QUIET TURBULENT EMOTIONS AND CLEAR AWAY COBWEBS OF DOUBT. FRIENDS WHO BRING BRIGHTNESS TO MY OVERCAST DAYS.

WITHIN THESE PAGES YOU WILL CATCH GLIMPSES OF SPECIAL PEOPLE WHO HAVE INCREASED MY AWARENESS OF ALL THAT IS BEAUTIFUL IN LIFE. YOU WILL UNDERSTAND WHY I SAY, "OUR BEING FRIENDS IS ANOTHER WAY OF KNOWING GOD."

PERHAPS YOU, TOO, WILL SENSE A SPARK OF RENEWED GRATITUDE FOR THE SPECIAL FRIENDS WHO ARE A NOSTALGIC PART OF YOUR PAST AND A CONTINUING PART OF YOUR FUTURE.

EACH GENUINE FRIENDSHIP IS FILLED WITH MANY WONDERFUL SURPRISES. I HOPE YOU ARE FINDING THEM!

Ruth Harms Calkin

A NOTE TO THE READER:

This collection of poetry contains a number of blank, lined pages. These are for you to use however you like—to record your thoughts, write a poem of your own, or recall a special memory. At the beginning of each set of journal pages are some questions to help you get started. If answering these questions helps you reflect and write, feel free to use them in this way. If not, disregard the questions and write whatever you wish. We hope that Ruth's poems, along with pages for your own thoughts, will combine to make this a book that is truly yours.

PART ONE

Friendship That Begins at Home

If home is what it is meant to be,

it is the place where we first learn to trust and to care.

Home and family teach us to share, to disagree,

to sacrifice, and to cherish the people we love.

True friendship begins in this special place

when we are very small, and as we grow up, our ability to be

a loving friend grows with us.

I remember so well the long-ago day
when my brother of seven years
sat at our kitchen table
to write a note to my parents.
He was anything but happy.
How dearly I loved him!
But often I hurt for him, too.
So many alibis!
So many collisions with trouble.

There had been an accumulation of things:
He hadn't picked up his clothes;
he'd tracked mud on the clean carpeting;
he had pinched his best friend
to see how loud he would scream.
One by one his privileges were taken away—
so he wrote:

"I don't want to live here anymore.
You are too strict.
So I'm running away.
P.S. If I get hungry
maybe I'll come back someday."

"Someday" didn't take long.
After an hour and twenty minutes,

the young prodigal came running home.
He was penitent. And hungry.
His hiding place had been dark.
There were tears. Also hugs.
And there was forgiveness.
He was welcomed home!

Oh, my Lord,
so often I too run away—
sometimes for days at a time,
when prayers seem unanswered,
for You say yes when I want You to say no
or no when I think I really need a yes.
When I want to go one way,
You point another direction.
Yet, when I run from You,
my world crumbles.
I feel desolate, lonely, fearful.
And I begin to hunger for Your presence.
I thirst for Your righteousness
and ache for restoration.
When finally I begin the long walk home, You are always waiting.
With wide open arms You welcome me.
Oh, my Father, there is no place like home!

Lorraine, Kansas, was known
as the City of Windmills.
How I loved having one
in our backyard.
If only I were brave enough
to climb the ladder!
If I reached the very top rung
I was sure I could touch the hand of God,
but I was too frightened to try.
Suddenly I had a thought:
My brother, two years younger than I,
was usually eager to please me.
If I could persuade him to climb to the top,
he could tell me how it felt to touch God!

I challenged and pleaded
until he finally agreed.
"I know God will help you," I assured him
(schemer that I was!).
He stepped on the first rung, the second,
the third and fourth.
"I'm so proud of you," I shouted.
Another rung, another and another,

almost to the last rung.
Then he looked down—and froze.

My mother heard the screams from the kitchen.
When she saw her young son on the ladder,
somehow she remained calm.
Her loving voice silenced the screams.
We called our neighbor.
In moments Johnnie was rescued.
He looked at me indignantly.
"You said if I climbed to the top
I could touch God, but I didn't even see Him!"

Oh, dear God!
So often You have used that windmill
to remind me
that I was simply trying too hard:
I want to climb the rung of performance,
the rung of good works, of prestige.
I find You, not by climbing,
but by kneeling
at the foot of the cross.

Her name was Jammie.
Quite unexpectedly one day
she came to live with us.
We never actually saw Jammie,
nor did we hear her.
My sister Rainy conveyed to our family
whatever information she considered worth sharing,
which wasn't much.
At times, when I sat on the couch,
Rainy requested that I make room for Jammie.
One day Rainy cried genuine tears;
Jammie had pinched her.

We lived in a large apartment building
in the city of Chicago.
The building housed seminary professors.
Since Dad was the only professor with a family,
we were cautioned not to disturb
the professors and their wives:
"Don't talk too loudly."
"Turn the radio down—quickly."
"Don't jump on the beds."
Rainy was not yet in school,
so it was lonely for her—until Jammie came.

Then a beautiful thing happened!
Another professor and his family
moved into an apartment close to ours.
Beth was Rainy's age.
Soon they were playing together;
they giggled and shared secrets
day after day.

One day our mother asked about Jammie.
"I haven't heard you talk about her at all."
Rainy looked at Mom in amazement.
"Mother! Didn't you know? Jammie died!"

Lord, I've thought of Jammie often.
Of course she died! At best she was
only a substitute for the real thing.
So often, I've created my own Jammies—
the yearning for things; a larger house;
prestige or popularity; a bigger bank account—
only to find all my Jammies sad substitutes
for the reality of the everlasting God.
Take my Jammies, Lord. All of them.
I long to experience anew
the *realty* of You.

At our house
we were dyed-in-the-wool note writers.
We grew up assuming
that all families everywhere wrote notes.
What else were scratch pads for?

We remember the notes our mother
tucked inside our lunch pails.
Three minutes after the lunch bell clanged
we'd grab our pails, and, sure enough—
nestled neatly between a juicy red apple
and a peanut butter sandwich
we'd find a personal note:
"I'll be praying for you during your test."
"Always remember how much we love you."
"We'll have your favorite dinner tonight."

Often we'd find notes in sweater pockets,
sometimes in the cookie jar
or next to our dinner plates,
often on our pillow tops.

One day, after diligently studying for a test—
one I was confident of passing—
I came home from school sobbing.
I had failed!
I would not be consoled.

That night I found a note on my pillow—
"We're so glad you are our daughter!"
Nothing about the test or the failure,
or "You'll do better next time."
Just the powerful assurance that I belonged.

Oh, God, thank You!
Your love is like that.
I am Your child.
You hold nothing against me.
Because of Jesus I have a perfect score.
I belong!

Home is a place filled with love.
It doesn't matter about the size or color.
It doesn't matter about the town it's in
or the street it's on.
It doesn't even matter if it's a parsonage.
It could be anywhere from New York
to San Francisco, or places in between.
It only matters that it's *your* home,
and that it makes you feel warm and secure.

Home is crunchy apple snacks
while you do your homework,
or warm chocolate chip cookies
that your mother baked.
Home is laughing at mealtime,
even if you have to be polite.
It's sitting in the middle of the floor
and kicking off your shoes.
It's having a friend stay all night.
Home is making fudge and licking the pan.
It's a hug from your mom and dad
when you've emptied the trash and made your bed.

Home is where you know the family rules
and obey them—even when you don't want to.
It's saying what you feel without being laughed at.
It's opening your own mail if you get any.
It's closing the door to your own room
and giggling over the phone
without having to explain what it's all about.
Home is a place where you know you're really loved
even when you're scolded . . . even when you cry.
Home is making up with your brother
after a long mad time.
It's listening to your dad tell stories
and talking to God together after dinner.
Home is the place where God lives, too.

When we were children
the dinner hour was always special.
There was a linen cloth on the table,
dinner plates edged in delicate blue,
and silver neatly placed.
Each of us had an initialed napkin ring.
Laughter, fun, and crazy stories
added spice to each meal.

One evening my father asked to be excused.
We paid little attention
as he walked toward the living room.
Mother was asking about our homework.
Suddenly we heard Dad's call:
"Children, come here! Come here!"
We all hurried to the living room.
"Dad, what do you want?"
(Maybe he had something for us—
a Milky Way candy bar—the best of surprises!)

My father asked us to sit on the floor
next to his comfortable chair.
"You came because I called?" he asked.

We were indignant.
"Dad, you know we always come when you call!"
"My dear children,
you could have come running or crawling,
skipping or hopping,
laughing or crying
—happy or sad.
The important thing is
you came when I called!
That's the way it is with Jesus.
He longs for us to come to Him.
No matter how we feel, we can always come.
He never turns us away."

No candy bar that night,
but Dad's illustration
left a tremendous impression on my young mind.
It has become more significant through the years.
I can come to Jesus without merit or apology;
I can come with my failure, my perplexity, my tears;
I can come in my joy or in my sorrow.
And even if I don't know what I feel,
He wants me to come!

WHAT WAS "HOME" LIKE WHEN YOU WERE GROWING UP? WHAT DID YOU LEARN ABOUT RELATIONSHIPS, ABOUT DEMONSTRATING LOVE, AND ABOUT SOLVING "PEOPLE" PROBLEMS? HOW DID HOME MOLD YOU INTO A PERSON WHO WOULD BECOME A FRIEND? WHO WAS YOUR VERY FIRST FRIEND?

Friendship often starts as a quiet melody. Through years of commitment,
of giving and receiving, of learning to be loyal, the quiet melody
becomes a majestic symphony.

R. H. C.

When I was in third or fourth grade,
my father became seriously ill.
The doctor's diagnosis
left little room for encouragement.
My mother's voice broke as, over the phone,
she requested special prayer.
My heart pounded with fear.
The thought of losing Dad was agonizing.
In my secret heart I knew only one solution:
Jesus could heal my father.

I closed my bedroom door
and knelt by my bed.
With an outburst of commitment I vowed:
"Dear Jesus, if You'll just make Daddy well,
I'll . . . I'll . . . go to Africa as a missionary!"
Tears bathed my face.
I was signing my life away.
I could think of nothing more fatal
than going to Africa, where lions and tigers
swallow people with one big gulp.
I had made the ultimate sacrifice.

Several weeks later my family was rejoicing.
Dad was well, and he'd soon be preaching again.
Life was normal for everyone but me.
I was on my way to Africa!
I secretly wondered
if it might have been better for Dad to die.
He would be in heaven, and I would be safe.

When I could no longer endure the struggle,
I spilled out my agony to my mother.
"God answered our prayer," she explained,
"because He still has work for your father to do—
not because He wanted to make you miserable.
Someday, if God wants you to go to Africa,
that's exactly what you'll want to do.
Let's just thank Him for being so wise and good.
Honey, do you want to pray first?"

Oh yes, I did! I breathed deeply
and prayed the most grateful prayer
a little girl had ever prayed.

Thank you, Mom and Dad,
for teaching me such
life-changing lessons.
From you I learned
that marriage is the day-by-day,
year-by-year togetherness
of two people who give each other
plenty of room to grow—
who recognize flaws
but accentuate virtues.
I learned the magic effect
of applauding each other—
of making allowances for each other.
Above all, I learned the deepening joy
of giving each other
all the love two hearts can hold.
Come to think of it,
I'm sure you would both say,
"First, God taught *us*."

We cannot say we've never quarreled
in all our years of marriage,
for we are very human, you and I.
There were times you said
my comments were silly and absurd.
I bit my tongue, and then I cried.
I hid where I thought
you'd never find me—
but you always did.
We've disagreed about some foolish things,
and even when we saw our stubborn pride,
we each insisted, "I was right."

But we have trust, and we have God;
and always we agree
that love is a ten-letter word:
c-o-m-m-i-t-m-e-n-t.
After every quarrel, at any time,
our laughter and forgiveness
throw us into each other's arms,
and we forget we ever quarreled!

TO MY DAUGHTER, BONNIE

I could tell you I treasure you
because you've brought gigantic love
and overflowing joy to my life.
Watching your growth has been a
gentle source of comfort through the years.
You have enlarged my capacity
to give thanks for the wonder of life.

I could tell you I treasure you
because you've stood by faithfully
in times of crucial family emergencies.
You have not turned away
from my honest endeavor to help you
put things in true perspective again
after some vicious inner struggles.

I could tell you I treasure you
because you've listened with your heart
as we've freely shared memories and goals—
as we've thanked God for the wide expansion
of your personal music ministry.

I could tell you I treasure you
because I see the reflection of you
in your three precious children.
You have taught them integrity and honesty.
As you've assured them of your love,
you've taught them to put God first—
even as they develop their own self-reliance.

I could tell you I treasure you
because you have given your husband
all the love and respect and honor
he so rightfully deserves.

But when it comes right down to it,
I'd rather tell you I treasure you
just because you're you—
my loving and radiant daughter.
You are God's special love-gift to me.

After my father's death,
I sat in his quiet office,
sorting through years of sermons
and personal journals.
A few tears fell on the pages.
My task was very personal,
and hundreds of memories
circled the room.

I was amazed, yet pleased,
when I began to compare
my journals with my father's.
Our groping and intense struggles,
our affirmations and confessions,
were so often curiously interlaced.
It would never have occurred to us
to share our journals while Dad was living.
Diaries, letters, journals,
even telephone calls were private.

Today I reflect upon my own record of life—
page after page of spiritual encounters.

Pain, anguish, questions, purging, joy,
discipline, insights, ecstasy, faith—
God's whispered secrets.

Suddenly the early beginning
has become very much alive:
A little girl, seven or eight,
hearing her father say,
"If you'll listen—really listen—
God will whisper secrets to you!"
My father had said something very
beautiful and strange.
I was breathless with wonder:
How did he know that God had secrets,
or that He would ever whisper them to us?

But as I sorted through my father's
careful recounting of
his inner life and journey,
it suddenly became very clear:
He, too, had heard God's secrets!

WHAT LESSONS ABOUT LIFE AND LOVE HAVE YOU LEARNED FROM
THE PEOPLE YOU HAVE LIVED WITH? WHO MODELED REAL FRIEND-
SHIP TO YOU? WHAT QUALITIES OF YOUR PARENTS, GRANDPARENTS,
BROTHERS, SISTERS, AUNTS, AND UNCLES DO YOU WANT TO BRING
TO YOUR RELATIONSHIPS NOW?

The happiest moments of my life have been in the flow

of affection among friends.

Thomas Jefferson

[PART TWO]

Gifts and Sacrifices

Sometimes we don't know

who our true friends are until the circumstances in our life

call for strength and resources that are beyond us.

Our dearest friends may be the most unassuming people, those who

work behind the scenes to support us. They may be the ones who make

sacrifices that no one else is willing to make.

They give to us when giving costs.

Miss Bailey!
My first-grade teacher.
Oh, how I loved her.
She was so beautiful!
I loved her gentle voice, her smile—
and her long, shiny hair.
One day I begged my mother
not to cut my bangs;
I wanted hair like Miss Bailey's.

We were learning to write—
not print, but actually *write*.
On a long sheet of paper I wrote my name
over and over again.
I knew that Miss Bailey
would stop at each desk
to examine our work.
When she approached my desk
my heart pounded.
I was sure she'd be pleased.

She looked down at the long sheet.
"I know you tried," she said,

"but you've spelled your name *Ruh . . . Ruh. . . .*
You left out the letter *t.*"
I burst into tears, my heart broken.
My one desire was to please Miss Bailey.
But, with all my sincere effort,
I had done it wrong.

Then a beautiful thing happened.
Miss Bailey took a clean sheet of paper
and held my small hand in hers.
With her guidance we wrote *Ruth . . . Ruth . . .*
neatly, and with much less effort.
My mistake no longer mattered.

I never think of Miss Bailey
without catching a fresh glimpse
of the Holy Spirit's work in my life.
"You try too hard, dear child.
You can't do it alone.
I am appointed to work through you."
Lord, when I obey, it's not only easier,
but I know You are pleased.

She lived in the most deprived section
of the vast and crowded city of New York,
where there was never enough of anything—
never enough food or clothing,
never enough warmth or shelter,
never enough compassion, concern, or hope.

But one day, to her glad amazement,
a benevolent young couple
invited her to spend a weekend at the seashore,
to experience a piece of life
she had never before known.

Hour by hour she stood digging
into the white sand with her bare feet.
She breathed deeply as the crashing waves
brushed against her small frame.
She looked at the vast expanse of water,
as far as she could possibly see.
And then, without warning, she began to sob.
She sobbed until there were no tears left.
For the first time in her entire life,
she saw something of which there was enough.

Oh, dear God,
please forgive
my small and limited concept of You.
I confess the times I've secretly felt cheated—
as though somehow You were not enough to satisfy
the deepest longings of my heart.
I need to learn and relearn that in You
there is enough faithfulness, enough love,
enough grace and mercy, enough joy!
Don't let me forget, dear Lord,
that You are forever my great *enough!*
And You are *enough* for every hungry heart
in all the wide world.
What can I do, where can I go
to make this known?
*"My concerned child,
start with your neighbors!"*

TWO GIFTS

On our piano there is a quaint gold vase.
In the vase there are two crimson rosebuds,
full of fragrance.
The vase is your birthday gift to me,
and, with all my heart,
I thank you for it.
Your cherished friendship
is God's personal gift to me.
With all my heart
I thank Him for you.

GOD WAS DELIGHTED

Several weeks ago
my husband and I again experienced
the joy of hospitality.
We invited to dinner
two couples we knew but slightly.
We wanted to know them better;
we were sure they would enrich our lives.
We asked them to dinner,
knowing that their circumstances
made it impossible for them to reciprocate.
Because they could not open
their homes to guests,
they were seldom invited to other homes.

The evening was wonderful!
Natural conversation—
and a very tender roast!
Also, some challenging discussions
and a lot of humor and spontaneous laughter.
We sang around the piano;
we shared childhood memories.

We talked about our backgrounds
and about spiritual concepts.
My husband and I wanted to pour the love of Jesus
into the lives of these two couples.
As we said good-night to each other,
we thanked God for the privilege
of knowing each other better.

While we were cleaning the kitchen
I asked, "Honey, do you think it went well?"
I'll never forget my husband's answer:
"I think God was delighted!"

MAKE ME A BETTER FRIEND

Lord, help me to be a better friend.
So often I'm too busy to listen attentively—
too busy to show genuine concern.
Curb my complaints; help me to be kind.
In some small way, may I bring encouragement
to someone whose heart may be breaking.
If my personal agenda is interrupted,
may I accept it as *Your* interruption—
an opportunity to open my heart
as well as the door of my home.
May I reach out with a smile,
and even a gentle hug.
Suddenly, as I talk to You, Lord,
I remember the old, old song:
"Be like Jesus, this my song,
in my home and in the throng."
Lord, keep me humming it all day long!

TAKE TIME TO REMEMBER THE PEOPLE WHO HAVE MADE SACRIFICES IN ORDER TO LOVE YOU. WHAT GIFTS DO YOU THINK WERE MOST COSTLY TO THEM? HAVE YOU EVER ACKNOWLEDGED THEIR GIFTS OF LOVE AND FRIENDSHIP? HOW CAN YOU THANK THEM NOW?

_____

_____

_____

_____

_____

_____

_____

I command you to love each other in the same way that I love you.
And here is how to measure it——the greatest love is shown
when people lay down their lives for their friends.

Jesus Christ, John 15:12-13

49

HIS IDEA

Several years ago I was invited
to speak to a group of young women
at a weekend mountain retreat.

"Lord, please surprise us with joy
this entire weekend."
That was my earnest prayer
as we drove over winding curves
on a cold, windy afternoon.
When we arrived at the campsite,
no other cars were in sight;
the cabins were dark.
Rain continued to fall in torrents.
I smiled as I prayed:
"Lord, is this Your idea
of surprising us with *joy?*"

Five or six minutes later,
another car arrived.
Three vivacious young women
called from their car:
"Hi! You must be the speaker.
We've been praying for you!
We're here to lead in worship."

That was my informal introduction
to Carolyn, Carol, and Katherine—
a wonderfully gifted trio
with the God-chosen name: *His Idea.*

Other campers arrived despite the rain.
Lights began to shine in cabins.
It took only a short time
to sense the power of God's *joy!*
Every song the trio sang that weekend
opened the door for my prepared messages.
Their music flowed with joyful freedom
as God's power flowed through them.
I was confident this was all "God's idea."
Deep commitments were made at the retreat.
Burdens were lifted, and prayers were answered.
The retreat ended with renewed surrender;
surely it was all His Idea.

My continuing friendship with the trio
is a treasured gift from God.
There is only one way to explain it:
Right from the beginning it *was* His Idea.

Lord, how could we have known
or imagined
that our early conversations
of hello, good-bye, and how-are-you-today?
would grow into a thousand tomorrows
of commitment and intimate sharing?
But now we do know
that our lives are richer,
our joy deeper,
our faith stronger,
because You have given us
in friendship
to one another.

A woman who is real
knows that in her family
she must sometimes back off
so that God can move in.

A woman who is real
continually builds a monument
of healthy memories
for her family.
She believes that memories establish values.
They create security;
they record a growing history
of God's great faithfulness.

A woman who is real
refuses to let her life be cluttered
with unconfessed guilts.
She keeps short accounts with God.
She guards her tongue,
knowing how quickly a little spark
can ignite a huge fire.

A woman who is real
listens well.

She is careful not to break
into an ongoing conversation
to tell her own story.

A woman who is real
knows that for thirty-two cents
and two minutes of time
she can write a note of one sentence:
"If it helps to know that somebody cares,
somebody does!"

A woman who is real
sheds the masks of pretense and sham;
there are no dark corners in her heart—
no credibility gap between who she is
and how she is toward others.

A woman who is real
feels no need
to "prove" her Christianity;
she herself is walking proof.

My husband taught me
a most helpful lesson about listening.
One day he came home from the office
weary, depleted, wanting to talk.
It had been an extremely difficult day,
and he needed to share the details.

"Honey, I want to hear you," I said,
"but I must dust the furniture
before the luncheon tomorrow.
So would you just follow me
from room to room and talk to me?"
We started in the living room.
While I dusted the stereo,
my husband stood next to me and talked.
When I dusted the bottom of the coffee table,
he leaned over and tried to talk.
(It was difficult to hear him.)
Just as I started to dust the piano
he grabbed my shoulders and turned me around.
"*Please* listen to me," he pleaded.
I was shocked. What did he mean?
I had heard almost every word he said.
"No, no! I mean—*listen with your heart!*"

I looked into his weary eyes
and saw that troubled expression.
I put the dust cloth away.
We both sat down, and I gave this love of mine
my undivided attention.
I didn't fold my arms or tap the arm of my chair.
I didn't look at my watch
but gazed intently and directly at him.
I *listened*.
After sharing the events of the day, he smiled.
"Thank you for caring enough to listen."
Our time together was good for both of us.

Something deep within me said,
That's what God wants — your listening heart.
Nothing will so steady and sensitize you
as much as a daily quiet time with the One
who longs for an intimate relationship with you.
I knew it was true.

PART OF THE GIFT

I heard today
of a decrepit native woman
who walked mile after mile
under the blistering sun
to bring a small gift of embroidery
to the missionary she deeply loved.
Hour after hour she trudged
over rough, rugged roads
clutching tightly her small gift.
Her weary body sagged;
her vision blurred;
her bare feet bled from the jagged rocks.

Grateful but overwhelmed,
the missionary wept.
The trembling old woman spoke softly:
"Please understand.
The walk is part of the gift."

My Lord,
my commitment to You is for life.
I give myself to You unreservedly
to do with me as You please.
But may I not forget
that the tears, the fears,
the strain and the pain,
the sunless days,
the starless nights
are all a part of the whole.
In my total commitment
I give full consent:
The walk is part of the gift.

(previously published in
Lord, It Keeps Happening . . .
and Happening)

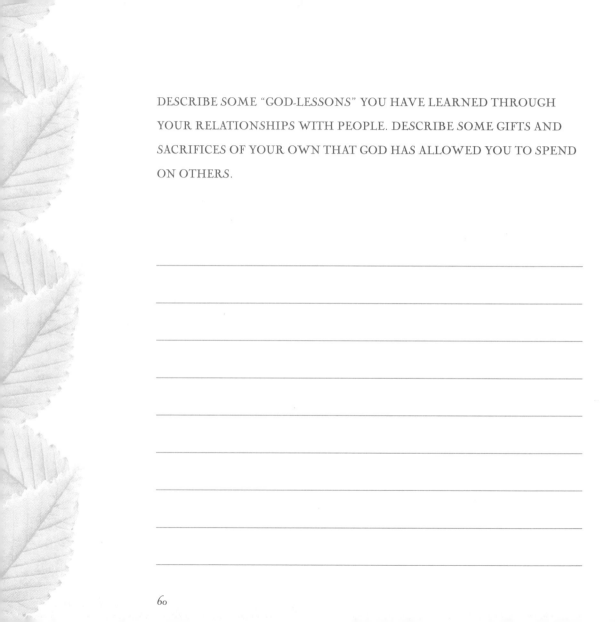

DESCRIBE SOME "GOD-LESSONS" YOU HAVE LEARNED THROUGH
YOUR RELATIONSHIPS WITH PEOPLE. DESCRIBE SOME GIFTS AND
SACRIFICES OF YOUR OWN THAT GOD HAS ALLOWED YOU TO SPEND
ON OTHERS.

If instead of a gem, or even a flower,
we should cast the gift of loving thoughts into the heart of a friend,
that would be giving as the angels give.

George MacDonald

[PART THREE]

Friends in Tough Times

No price can be placed upon friends

who stay with us through absolutely everything.

When most people become weary from listening to our

troubles, a friend keeps asking, "How are you—really?"

When trials make us brittle and dismal,

a friend continues to open her heart and let us in.

Friends are God's safe places on earth.

MY JOB DESCRIPTION

If I am able to speak and to write
and to entertain friends,
to listen to their serious problems—
but do not *live* what I write
and what I say
and do not follow the careful advice
I pour out to others,
then all my written and spoken words
blow away like sand,
and I am nothing more
than a well-polished showpiece.

Jeff is my friend.
We've been friends
since he was eight years old.
He was my piano student
many years ago.
I can still envision him:
freckles covering his nose,
crewcut,
a smile that reached
from one ear to the other.
Excellent student—
just one problem:
He loved to improve
on the master composers
by rendering his own arrangements.
(Evidently it paid off;
today Jeff is working on his doctorate
in the field of music and drama.)

One particular lesson day
he played every piece accurately;

he didn't "rearrange"
a single note or line.
"Well," he said during his lesson,
"how's *that* for a miracle!"
"Excellent, Jeff! I'm proud of you!"

One more book to tackle.
More mistakes than I could count.
"Oh, Jeff, *why?*"
Boyish grin.
"I just blew the miracle!"

My one consolation, dear God!
In all the eons of history
You have never once
blown a miracle.
You never will.
I praise You for that!

My husband and I were ecstatic.
We were spending our
twenty-fifth wedding anniversary
in beautiful Hawaii.
After we checked into the Kuilima Hotel
on the north shore of Oahu,
a brown-skinned Hawaiian bellman
carried our luggage to our room.
Although we were anxious to unpack,
we discovered the bellman wanted to talk.
His work was finished for the day.

Then suddenly, to our amazement,
he asked, "Could you talk about God?"
Indeed we could!
We shared the John 3:16 story—
how God had sent His only Son
to die for our sinful world,
how He had a plan for each of us,
how He loved us with an everlasting love.
We spoke as simply as we could.
We wanted so much for him to understand.

He said, "My wife is picking me up.
Could you tell her about Jesus, too?
I'll go get her."
What a way to celebrate our anniversary!
We hadn't even unpacked our luggage,
and here we were
telling a bellman and his wife
how to accept Jesus Christ as their Savior.
They knelt by our bed
and surrendered their lives to the One
who had obviously arranged our visit.

After our vacation we wondered if Alan and Pam
would follow through on their decision.
We didn't wonder long. They wrote to us.
They sent us a picture of their baby boy.
"We will tell him about Jesus," they said.

Often we wondered—
were we friends or acquaintances?
Well, when the result is two new Christians,
wouldn't you say we were friends?

Lord, if life is to have meaning,
we must discover that
when we face our own personal volcanos,
when betrayal brings deep depression,
and relationships that seemed "forever"
are suddenly severed
without an explanation . . .

When there is nothing but emptiness
and loneliness and despair,
when one disappointment follows another,
and still another,
when dreams grow faint and finally die,
when there is more darkness than light . . .

What finally brings peace is this:
It could not have happened, God,
if You had not permitted it;
and because You permitted it,
You will turn every cross
into a crown.
God, we can believe You for this!

All day long the sun had hibernated
in the somber clouds.
A winter wind weaved around the corners
of our many windows.
A deep chill had lodged within my heart
until I heard the ring of our doorbell.
I opened the door, and there you stood
with your cheerful smile
and your merry eyes.
Even before our friendly hug
I felt wrapped in joy
and blessed from head to foot.

WHAT LESSONS HAVE FRIENDS TAUGHT YOU ABOUT GETTING
THROUGH LIFE'S MORE DIFFICULT TIMES? HOW HAS GOD'S
FRIENDSHIP STRENGTHENED YOU FOR YOUR JOURNEY?

Friends can reveal the secrets in their souls without fear

of being censored or betrayed.

R. H. C.

Lord God,
as I sit here quietly
with my friend of many years,
make me, I pray, a gentle transmitter
of Your calming peace.
In her newborn pain,
You alone can sustain her.
You alone can stabilize her.
Use me, I pray, to show her
how eager You are
to be all she needs—
not tomorrow, Lord,
not next week,
but today,
now, this very moment!

Her name is Laurie.
The minute she opened our front door
I knew she had been crying.
Her blue eyes were red and swollen.
She placed her music on the piano
and proceeded to blow her nose.

Through years of teaching I have discovered
an amazing correlation
between a heartache and a piano lesson.
A hectic morning, a family quarrel,
lack of preparation for a test,
almost any seeming calamity
can play havoc at lesson time—
even after a week of practice.

"Laurie, I have a great idea," I said,
as I tilted her quivering chin.
"Maybe you'll feel better
if you tell me about the tears."
So it began—the story of a miserable day.

She had been late for school;
she had forgotten her lunch;
she had lost a library book;
when she fell and skinned her knee,
some of the kids laughed.
All day long nothing but trouble!

We talked about trouble—hers and mine.
We talked about the trouble
many of our friends were having.
When I saw the familiar smile again,
I knew we were ready for a lesson.
But before placing her hands on the keyboard,
Laurie drew a deep breath.
With thoughtful concern she said,
"I guess the whole world has an ache in its heart."

Yes, Laurie, yes!
And Jesus Christ
is the only One
who can heal that ache.

STEPHANIE

More than anything else,
she wanted to play the piano.
Her mother called to ask
if I would give her lessons.
"I must tell you one thing,"
her mother said.
"Stephanie is fighting
an advancing malignancy.
She has only one arm.
Her left arm has been amputated.
Her future is critical."

I was startled.
How could I teach a little girl
with only one arm to play the piano?
But the mother's words kept echoing . . .
"More than anything else,
she wants to take lessons."

*Dear God, I don't know how it will work,
but surely I can teach her the music of love.*

On her first lesson day
she came with her new beginner's book.

Her eyes sparkled. She could hardly wait!
Week after week Stephanie was a delight
as we sat at the piano together
learning notes, playing melodies—
she with her right hand, I with my left.
"I'm Mrs. Treble," she often told me.
"You're Mr. Bass."
It was a happy joke between us—
the kind that called for giggles.

One day after a lesson Stephanie said,
"We're really good together!
But you know what?
I could never do it alone."
I learned an incredible lesson, Lord.
When I follow Your instructions,
we make beautiful music together.
But I could never do it alone!

Stephanie is with You now, Lord.
What a joy it must be for her
to play with both hands!

Friendship:
The beautiful moment
when our lives touched
and God whispered,
"Your friendship is my gift."

Friendship:
A listening heart,
a shoulder to lean on,
a special kind of caring
that makes being together
a special kind of day.

Friendship:
Believing in each other,
understanding each other,
being loyal to one another,
confiding dreams and goals
and very personal secrets—
knowing that,
whatever the future holds,
our todays are creating
tomorrow's precious memories.

Oh, dear God, thank You!
There is no hurt, no offense, no agony
too great for You to heal.
Whatever the demeaning injustice,
the love of Your Son can withstand it.
When we ask for the gift of forgiveness,
You always say yes!

Forgiveness simply means
a deliberate release of an offense.
We *choose* to forgive.
We accept, we release, we drop the charges—
just as You dropped *all* charges against us.
The enabling power comes from You.

Forgiveness frees us from our subjectivity.
We no longer wince or wallow in self-pity.
We may *remember* at times,
but we are confident that You are weaving
every memory into Your glorious pattern.
Your redemptive love covers our memories!
When we genuinely forgive,
we discover that forgiveness
is a beautiful word—
an exceptionally beautiful word!

HOW HAVE TROUBLES AND BURDENS HELPED YOU TO BUILD MORE
DEPTH INTO YOUR RELATIONSHIPS? WHEN IS IT TOUGH TO BE A
GOOD FRIEND?

_____

_____

_____

_____

_____

_____

_____

_____

Friendship means unconditional acceptance, even when
we cannot give unconditional approval.

R. H. C.

[PART FOUR]

Special Friends I Have Known

Each friend we make introduces

a whole new facet to our life. Through other people

we learn about new celebrations and sorrows, different vocations,

gifts, and tasks. And each person who loves us

offers us God in a fresh new face.

Do you remember the first time we met?
Somehow, ours was an "instant friendship."
Friendship doesn't often begin with a very first smile—
but it happened to us.

There are so many reasons
I treasure your friendship.
The first time we met
it quickly was obvious
that you were truly God's person.
You let God put things into your life
or take them out—just as He wished.
You have fought a tremendous health battle;
yet, through sleepless nights,
through strain and struggle and weariness,
you have given God first place in your life.
Always you say *yes* to His quiet voice
as He continues to conform you
to the image of His dear Son.

I have learned so much from you;
you have left a permanent imprint on my life.

It is just as easy for us to share sorrow
as it is to share joy,
just as easy to share tears
as it is to share laughter.
A friend is one you can trust completely;
God has given us that trust.

As I pray for you day after day,
I wait patiently for God to surprise you
with the wonderful gift of health.
All of us wait and pray together:
your husband who cherishes and adores you,
your family for whom you have been a touchstone
of security and unconditional love,
your friends who are always there for you.

I want to say it once more:
I thank God for His gift to us.
As we have so often said and written,
ours is a "forever" friendship!

Lord, we can never thank You sufficiently
for the changes You are making in our lives
as we read Your Word aloud
from three different versions
and pray together every Wednesday morning.
These past three years Your powerful Word
has challenged and delighted us.
The more we read, the more we find.
You startle us with fresh insights.

Our love for You is deeper,
our friendship ever sweeter.
You have increased our compassion and concern
as we pray for those on our lists:
our families, friends, neighbors,
our churches, our ministries, our society.
We pray for those who need You desperately.
We pray for our sick and frightened world.

You have shown us that prayer is a dialogue.
We are learning to *listen* with our hearts.
We rejoice that we can bring *everything* to You:

our needs, heart-secrets, weaknesses,
as well as our joys, praise, and gratitude.
Your Word tells us You delight
in the prayers of Your children.

Lord, You have answered so many requests.
Some answers have come quickly—others slowly.
We continue to pray boldly, expectantly,
as we wait for answers still to come.
We need never pass through jumbled traffic
to reach Your Throne Room.
All the signal lights are green.

We are learning the great value of intercession.
We see anew that the safest place
in all the world is the center of Your will.
We see daily our personal need
for discipline! obedience! consistency!
In countless ways You are transforming us
as we consistently pour out our hearts to You.
We praise You, Lord! We praise You!

I stand in line with my cart of groceries.
The box boy fills my sacks.
He carries them to the car.
I learn that his name is Ray.
He's friendly, courteous—and fast.
"Ray, where do you go to church?"
He smiles. "Well, I don't go anymore.
Just sort of changed my priorities."
"Ray, I teach a class of seniors on Sunday."
"Oh, yeah? I'm a senior."
"Really, Ray? Maybe you could visit our church.
I'd like for my class to meet you.
You've got a great smile!"
"Thanks! Maybe I will someday."

In a week or so we need more groceries.
I see Ray again. He remembers me.
We talk on the way to my car.
I ask about his family, his future plans.
I enjoy talking to him.
One Sunday Ray shows up in my class.

I'm overwhelmed. I prayed that he'd come,
but my faith wasn't that strong.

Ray stays after class.
I introduce him to other kids.
He knows some of them from school.
I want him to meet my husband.
"Come to our house for a Coke, Ray."
To my great delight he comes.
The three of us spend several hours together.
He says he wants to know Jesus. Amazing!
I thank God again and again.

Ray meets a fine girl. They marry.
Before they move to San Diego he writes a note:
"I never knew what it meant to be a Christian
before I knew you and your husband. Thanks!
I hope we'll always be friends."

LESSON FROM CRAIG

He came for his lesson
with his brand-new piano book—
his *second* book, in fact.
Before he opened to the first page
he asked, "How many books
do I have to finish before
it's time to quit?"

Lord, I understand Craig's question.
I am *so* prone to ask,
"How many more lessons must I learn
before I've learned enough?"
And then I remember
that growth is a process—
a time-consuming process,
and God is not finished with me yet.

I love what William Barclay,
the great Bible scholar,
wrote on all his letters
during his eighty-fifth year:

"William Barclay, eighty-five years old
and still growing."

Lord, I suppose
when I'm eighty-five years old
You'll tell me
there are still more lessons
for me to learn.
However, I doubt that Craig
is ready to hear that!

I open the front door, and on the doorstep
I find a Coke bottle filled with fresh flowers.
A tiny note says, "Have a happy day!"
I recognize the writing. The gift is from Sheila.
A week or so later the mailman leaves a card.
I read: "You are so special to me."
(I love being special to Sheila.)
The other day I found chocolate chip cookies
at our door. Huge cookies! Delicious!
Sheila must double the batch every time.
Once I found a pumpkin. Another time a balloon.
The phone rings. Sheila's voice sparks my day.
It never stops. It's a joy called *friendship*.
We met at church a long time ago.
We didn't know exactly why we wanted to be friends.
We just knew we did.

Sheila was my piano student years ago.
Today she has music students of her own.
She teaches a weekly Bible class for women.
Lives are being transformed.

She takes joy in her husband,
her children, her granddaughters.
When we have breakfast or lunch together,
there is nothing we can't talk about.
We laugh together. Sometimes we cry together.
Sheila has the gift of touching troubled hearts.
Her home extends its arms and says
"welcome!"
Once inside the door,
you know God lives there, too.

Friendship!
It can happen any time
and anywhere,
but it's always blessed
when God arranges it.

PINKI

I met her just a short time
after she graduated from high school.
She was young, pretty, and just a bit shy.
She often covered her shyness
with a contagious laugh.
Somehow, right from the beginning,
I sensed we would be friends.
She came to our home once, twice . . .
eventually she came again and again.
She shared her family background,
her dreams, her disappointments.
She shared her deepest desires.
Together we shared the priceless gift of time.
One day she said pensively,
"More than anything in the world,
I want to be a nurse. I never lose the desire."
However, she had been told by a doctor
that she probably didn't have the physical stamina
for all the rigors of professional nursing.
I remember saying, "Pinki, if it is God's plan
for you to be a nurse, He'll remove every obstacle."

Oh, the joy and excitement we felt
the day she began her training.
With amazing insight
she absorbed quickly all she was taught.
She won honor after honor.
After graduation she was employed
by the very doctor who had questioned
her physical stamina.
Her patients loved and trusted her.
The entire hospital staff admired her.
For over thirty years her service
included all of our family,
as well as the families of close friends.
Her deep compassion buoyed her strength.
Always she was there for us. She still is.
Pinki! A delightful name.
Pinki! Another name for friendship.

WHO HAVE BEEN SPECIAL FRIENDS TO YOU OVER THE YEARS? WHAT
UNIQUE GIFTS DID THEY BRING YOU? IF YOU COULD TALK TO THEM
NOW, WHAT WOULD YOU SAY?

Tychicus, a much loved brother and faithful helper in the Lord's work, will

tell you all about how I am getting along. I am sending him

to you for just this purpose. He will let you know how we are,

and he will encourage you.

Paul the apostle, Ephesians 6:21-22

I love being friends with you!
Year after year
you give yourself
in so many ways
to those who need you:
your husband, your family, your friends,
the many students you counsel.
There is no pretense in you;
no masks cover your heart.
You run to win;
you take the bitter with the sweet;
you keep on trusting
when you haven't a single clue
what God's next move will be.

I love being friends with you!
When life has been painful,
when your plans have shattered,
you've thanked God
that He has better plans.

As you walk with Him,
He brings fresh dawns
and new songs.
You exemplify joy and trust and love.

I love being friends with you!
You have taught me so much
about genuine caring.
There is a no-matter-what quality
in your commitment.
How pleased God must be
that He created you
as He continues His unique plan
for your consistent life.
I love being friends with you!

CARMEN DOROTHY

She cared for me when I was a patient
in the tuberculosis sanatorium in Oregon.
I had never known a kinder nurse.
Her smile added sunlight to my dismal room.
She did all she could to make the long,
dreary days more pleasant.
One day when I was pushing back tears, she said,
"Tears are a wonderful release. Let them come!"

But one day an X ray revealed
that she herself had contracted tuberculosis.
No, oh no! The nurse I so dearly admired
would now be a patient instead of my nurse.
It seemed utterly impossible. So wrong.

We were rooms apart from each other.
So we wrote letters. Long letters.
We shared feelings. Heartaches.
Our hopes and our longings.
Somehow we always knew
we were there for each other.

One day I wrote a long, long letter
telling Carmen Dorothy about Jesus—
how He loved her, how He had died for her,
how she could know Him.

"Let's set a time.
At ten o'clock I hope you will
invite Jesus into your heart.
He loves you so much.
He wants you to trust Him!"

She answered with her own letter:
"I did just as you said.
I accepted Jesus. I know I belong to Him now.
For the first time in weeks I cry
because I'm very happy!"

I was discharged from the sanatorium
while my friend was still a patient.
It broke my heart to leave her.
Day and night I prayed for her.
Several months later a note came from her nurse:
"Carmen Dorothy died last night.
She asked me to tell you
how much she loved God—and you."

She was my nurse—
she became my friend;
I know I'll see her again!

A few days before her death
it was necessary to take my mother
to the hospital—after caring for her
in her home for a number of months.
We did not have the hospital equipment
that was needed as her body weakened.
Hour after hour I stood by her bed,
hoping for just some slight response—
just one more precious thing to remember.

One day as I waited,
our dear friend Muriel walked into the room.
"Oh, Muriel, I'm so sorry,
but Mother is no longer conscious.
She won't even know you're here."

"Ruth, I didn't come to visit your mother.
I came to be with you. I know you are hurting,
and I'm hurting with you.
I love your mother, too."
We stood together by the bed.

We talked—not serious talk—
just the kind of conversation
that is part of friendship during sorrow.

I noticed that Muriel didn't quote Romans 8:28,
as so many had done. She knew I believed
that wonderful promise, but she was sure
God could *whisper* it to me
far better than she could *say* it.
She didn't stay long—just long enough
to give the support I needed.
Her parting words were, "Isn't it wonderful—
His grace really *is* sufficient!"

Oh, God, what a beautiful gift:
the gift of a sensitive heart—
to be there at the right time,
to say the right thing,
to prove the real meaning of caring—
that's what sensitivity is all about!

Ours is a friendship
that grows richer through the years.
You've put a song in our heart,
and the song just keeps singing.
Our relationship is a growing history
of God's special gift to us.

So many memories . . .
your beautiful wedding
and your glistening happiness;
the honor you gave my husband
by asking him to perform the ceremony
in the candlelit sanctuary;
the incredible joy you gave me
in requesting that I accompany
your lovely mother down the wedding aisle.
"You are my mentor mother," you explained.

More memories . . .
the quiet dedication ceremony
after your first precious son was born.
Members of both families were present,
but Jay slept peacefully through it all!

It didn't matter. God knew your desire
to commit Jay to His loving care.
Several years later,
holding Jay's brother
for the very first time.
Derek! The adorable blue-eyed newcomer
who asked for nothing more
than loving care.
Watching love flow from both of you
at the amazing wonder of it all.

Several weeks ago, after enjoying
dinner in your spacious home,
we were reminded once more
that when God has first place
in the hearts of a devoted family,
He simply cannot be hidden.
Even the walls seem to sing His praises.

TO PAULA

You were five years old
and bright and perky
the day your mother and grandmother
brought you to our home
to talk about piano lessons.
Your eyes were very blue,
your hair was blonde,
and you looked at me directly
with every word we spoke.
I loved you immediately,
but I certainly had no idea
how far a journey our friendship would take us.

You make me think deeply about God.
You cause me to test my personal beliefs.
You throw out insights that challenge me.
In both of our lives there
have been emotional battles
and stormy nights,
but as we've shared the storms,
God has sent His rainbow every time.

Your thoughtfulness has taken many forms.
You've sent gourmet recipes
with special seasonings and spices.
You've introduced me to authors
whose books have expanded my life.
You've given me lasting gifts.
You dress your home with design and charm,
and when you open your door,
you always open your heart.
We have talked for hours at a time,
and yet we always have more to share.

I thank you for so many things,
but thank you most of all
for strengthening my conviction
that God's way is always best,
regardless of the test.

TRY TO WRITE DOWN A MEMORY THAT REPRESENTS WHAT EACH
SPECIAL FRIENDSHIP HAS MEANT TO YOU.

_____

_____

_____

_____

_____

_____

_____

_____

_____

I no longer call you servants, because a master doesn't confide in his servants. Now you are my friends, since I have told you everything the Father told me. You didn't choose me. I chose you.

Jesus Christ, John 15:15-16

PART FIVE

Our Greatest Friend

All love leads us eventually to the God of love.

And every true friend guides us deeper into our friendship with that

One who knows us more intimately than anyone else can.

Unlike human friends, who can growweary and fail us, our Friend

in heaven is with us always, constant in love and understanding,

and offering us the grace to meet every challenge.

God, Your Word says,
"And Abraham believed God,
and he was called the friend of God."
Lord, I long for a faith so strong
that you and I may become best friends!

(previously published in
Tell Me Again, Lord, I Forget)

At the church my father pastored
in Burlington, Iowa,
a special week had been planned
for the express purpose
of ministering to non-Christians.
On the night of the first service,
just before we left for church,
my father took me aside for a few minutes.

"Honey, when you're a little older
I know you'll want to give your heart to Jesus,
but you are still very young,
and I want you to really understand
what it means to follow Jesus.
Tonight I hope you'll listen carefully
to the guest minister.
When we get home, we'll talk about the sermon."
My father's motive was honest and sincere.
Knowing my tender heart and my quick willingness
to accept *any* invitation, *any* time,
he wanted to protect me
against an emotional experience
that might have little or no significance later.

I trusted Dad completely. I intended to obey him.
But as I listened to the sermon, I *knew* it was for me.

Jesus died for me! He loved and forgave me!
He wanted *me* to "open my heart"
and belong to Him forever! Why must I wait?
I felt sad and very lonely.
How old did I have to be?
How could I say no to Jesus? He died for *me*!

I glanced toward the pulpit.
Through my choking tears I saw my father.
He was smiling at me and nodding his head.
I literally rushed down the aisle.
I was running on a cloud,
but the cloud couldn't keep up with me.
My father came to meet me.
"Oh, Daddy, now I can obey Jesus and you, too!"

On Easter of that year
my father baptized me.
Never have I doubted the reality of that night.
Dad often said later,
"How unwise it is for us to attempt
to determine God's timing!"

Thank You, my Lord,
for speaking to my young heart
that long-ago night of all nights!

MY HEART NEEDS YOU

Oh, dear God, how my heart needs You—
the deep inner cavern of me,
the secret places,
ones of confusion and fear.
Help me believe that Your darknesses
are surely not Your goals.
They are simply tunnels
to get me to a more beautiful place.

The lights will soon be dimmed,
and morning will bring the daily routine.
Lord, may tonight bring hours of quiet sleep.
I rest on the pillow of blessed assurance:
He is silently planning, in love, for me.

GROWTH THAT IS REAL

Oh, dear God,
I don't want to be
a plastic flower
without life,
fragrance,
growth.

Transplant me, if You must.
Root me, cultivate me,
clear the weeded areas.
Send rain, send the sun,
even storm clouds, dear Lord,
until I am like a watered garden,
daily delighting Your heart
with growth that is real!

Janet and I quickly discovered that
we didn't need time to get acquainted.
As we followed the pull of our hearts,
it was as though we'd always known each other.
The years have solidly bonded us
as we've laughed and wept together—
as we've challenged each other to grow.

One day, while sharing our wistful longings,
I told her how my many years
of keeping a prayer journal
had been a tremendous stimulus
in my personal encounter with God.
She listened thoughtfully,
asked question after question.
Before we said good-bye
I shared bits of my journaling with her.

Through the fast-changing years
she has become a wife, a mother,
and a highly respected school principal.
Her days are charged with responsibilities.

That's why a quick flame of gratitude flared
when I read her recent note:
"Ruth, perhaps your greatest contribution
to my life came the day
you taught me to write my thoughts
and longings to God—then to listen
as He revealed His answers
through His Word.
Thank you for a very special gift
that will have lasting and
growing fulfillment
all the days of my life."

O God, thank you
for the beautiful growth
I've seen in Janett hrough the years.

My Lord,
I have made three overwhelming discoveries
regarding Your reliable faithfulness:

The first:
You will never let me go—*never!*
I may fall flat on my face.
I may resist until I feel exhausted,
but absolutely nothing can separate me
from Your matchless love.
I am graven on the palm of Your hand.

The second:
You will never let me down—*never!*
You are forever faithful,
even when I am faithless.
You simply cannot deny Yourself.
"I will never leave you nor forsake you."
This is Your positive promise.

The third:
You will never let me off—*never!*
Whenever I give in to temptation,

when I stubbornly rebel and disobey,
when I determine to have my own way—
You say with all the love of Your Father-heart,
"I love you too much
to excuse your disobedience."
Your Word makes it very clear:
"Whom I love I chasten."

You are determined to bless me;
You are anxious to use me;
You are eager to show me Your kindness;
You are glad to teach me the proper paths;
but You *must* have access to all of my heart.
You will allow my guilt to become a burden
until conviction comes,
then confession, then cleansing,
and finally renewed commitment!

My Lord,
may David's prayer be my prayer:
"Turn me away from wanting
any plan other than Yours."

WHAT QUALITIES OF FRIENDSHIP ARE ALSO QUALITIES THAT MARK
GOD'S RELATIONSHIP TO YOU? DESCRIBE GOD AS THOUGH YOU
WERE TRYING TO INTRODUCE ONE FRIEND TO ANOTHER.

_____

_____

_____

_____

_____

_____

_____

And so it happened just as the Scriptures say:

"Abraham believed God, so God declared him to be righteous."

He was even called "the friend of God."

James 2:23

Oh, God, thank You!
I know it is true—
every disappointment
or frustrated desire
is never the final act.
It is simply an experience
to draw me even closer
to Your ever-loving heart.

Lord, You know how the sermon yesterday
really sparked my thinking:
How do I draw near
to dwell in Your holy presence?
How do I take the routine day
with its many distractions
and find a place of restful solitude
sitting at Your feet?
How do I step out of the hubbub
and into the holy?
The questions are mine, Lord;
the answers must be Yours.

My husband's prayer this morning
aroused a quick response in my heart.
"Lord, You promised
to be with us always—
right down to the last minute."

The last minute . . .
When will it be?
What will determine it?
An accident?
A heart attack or plane crash?
A war?

The last minute . . .
While driving?
Vacationing? Playing tennis?
At work? Visiting friends?
Eating dinner? Raking leaves?

The last minute . . .
During a church service?
Celebrating a birthday?
Watching television?
Grocery shopping?

The last minute . . .
In a hospital room?
During surgery?
In a convalescent home?
While sleeping?

Nobody knows but You, dear Lord;
but we do know
You will be there,
holding us close
to Your loving heart,
right down to the very last minute.

How I love the words
of the apostle Paul:
"I haven't learned all I should even yet,
but I keep working toward that day
when I will finally be
all that Christ saved me for.
No, I am still not all I should be,
but I am bringing all my energies to bear
on this one thing: Forgetting the past
and looking forward to what lies ahead,
I strain to reach the prize
for which God is calling me"
(Philippians 3:12-14, paraphrase).

What a tremendous encouragement!
Paul, who knew Jesus Christ so intimately,
whose consuming desire was to please Him,
who endured illness, imprisonment,
shipwreck, beatings, mockery, and heartache
all for the sake of Christ—
this very same Paul confessed
he hadn't "arrived."
God was still growing him!

I see again, dear Lord,
while my conversion
took but a moment,
my growth takes an entire lifetime.
In Your great wisdom and knowledge
You anticipate the finished *product*
while You lovingly take me through
the long, long *process*.

My wonderful Lord,
through all the incredible years
I have been Your child,
I have seen it happen again and again:
When I walk in the fullness of Your ways,
You pour upon me so lavishly
the fullness of Your promises!

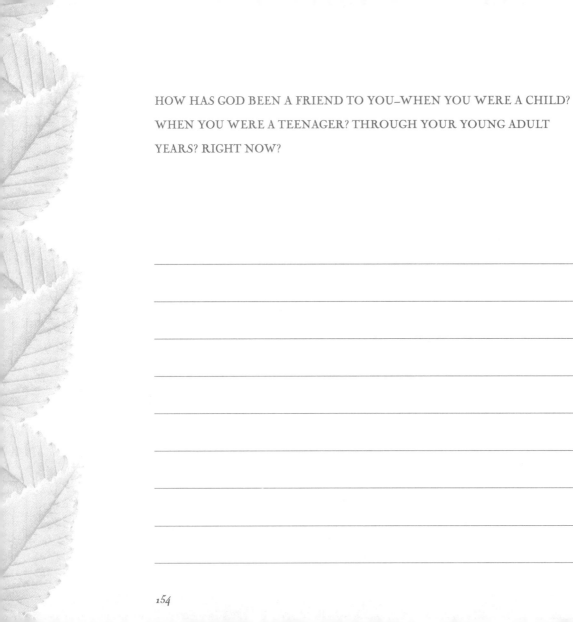

HOW HAS GOD BEEN A FRIEND TO YOU—WHEN YOU WERE A CHILD?
WHEN YOU WERE A TEENAGER? THROUGH YOUR YOUNG ADULT
YEARS? RIGHT NOW?

I am convinced that nothing can ever separate us from
[God's] love. Death can't, and life can't. The angels can't,
and the demons can't. Our fears for today, our worries about tomorrow,
and even the powers of hell can't keep God's love away.

Paul the apostle, Romans 8:38

Lord, I love this fresh April morning!
The sky is brilliantly blue.
Shiny fresh buds are forming
on the trees in our parkway.
Lord, will You walk with me today,
as You've done so often before?

You've walked with me
over rough and dangerous roads,
over narrow, winding paths.
When my heart was wrapped in darkness,
You've walked with me
through miles of parched wilderness.
You've walked with me
through emotional earthquakes
that uprooted my total being.

But, Lord, if You'll walk with me today,
I'm confident You'll discover
that my faith has quietly grown.
I'm no longer so frenzied and fearful.

Our walks have changed me completely.
Never once did You leave my side.

On this fresh spring morning
my heart overflows with one desire:
As we walk I want to praise
the majesty and the splendor of You.
Will You walk with me, Lord?

(previously published in
Keep Me Faithful)